© Neil Hawley-Evans 2002

10 9 8 7 6 5 4 3 2 1

CW01468336

Neil Hawley-Evans asserts the moral right to _____ of this work

A catalogue record for this book is available from the British Library

ISBN 0–9543564–0–3

Published by
BUZZTALKS™
PO Box 1560
Stoke-on-Trent
ST12 9BX

Printed in Great Britain by
Panda Press (Stone) Ltd

(BUZZTALKS is a registered trademark)

Contents

Chapter   Page

Introduction   3

1   Whose Life is it anyway?   4

2   Taking Stock   8

3   Success   11

4   Goals   14

5   Affirmations   19

6   Money   24

7   Positive Action   28

8   Dealing with Resistance   31

9   Belief   35

10   Desire   38

11   Momentum   41

12   The Power of Questions   44

13   Body Talk   47

14   Mind Your Language   50

15   When Will I Get to the Jam?   54

16   Banana Theory   57

17   Keep on, Keeping on   59

Index   62

INTRO

Are you happy and contented? Is you life really 'working' for you?

Do you wake up each morning full of optimism, enthusiasm and purpose for the day ahead? Or are you plagued by nagging doubts? Feel like you are going nowhere fast? Constantly under – performing in everything that you do? No idea what you want to achieve in life? Tired of seeing everything that you attempt, fail miserably? Is your life in a rut?

A rut was once described to me by a good friend, as a grave with two open ends. And when you go, as you inevitably will, there will be a mark of your existence which will start with the year of your birth, followed by a dash, and then the year of your death. Let me put a question to you. What will your dash represent? Will it be a life lived without passion, direction or fulfilment, locked in the bitterness and frustration of knowing that you deserved better? Will you have gone to your grave with your music still within you, unheard by the world at large?

Or will you have strived in your every waking moment to move towards the achievement of your ultimate dreams and goals? Will you shuffle off from this mortal coil, safe in the knowledge that you gave it your all? 110%? You could do no more?

Most of us are not going to climb Everest or circumnavigate the globe single-handed. Life isn't like that. Yet I believe we will all face our own distinct challenges. Our own personal 'Everest'. This book is designed as a practical guide to help you to recognise those challenges, to define what success means to you, and to put a strategy in place to help you achieve more in all areas of your life. So here it is. The ultimate guide to defining and achieving success in your life.
And remember.......

If you want to, then you will.

WHOSE LIFE IS IT ANYWAY?

How is your life working for you right now?

Are you on track with everything that you set out to be, have and do? Or are you stuck in a rut, with no means of escape doing the same old same, day in, day out, week in, week out? Are you living your life…? Or are you living a life that meets the needs of other people? Friends, family, work colleagues?

The good news is that you can change anything you want to in your life. Make a decision to live your life. The challenge is to make that initial step and take action to change your life. You cannot discover new oceans unless you have the courage to lose sight of the shore. If you always do what you've always done, then it will come as no surprise to you, that you will always get, what you have always got. As Edward de Bono says —

'You can't dig a hole in a different place by digging the same hole deeper.'

The problem is that we are human beings. As human beings we are naturally resistant to change, preferring instead to repeat familiar and comfortable behaviour patterns. Once these patterns are created, and we see that no harm will come of us, then we prefer and choose to stay within the limits of these self-regulated 'comfort zones'. It's almost as if we have cordoned off an area around ourselves with tape, and restrict ourselves to a limited area. You know what's coming though, don't you? It's a fact that, if we want to change, move forward and develop in our lives, then there is a fair chance that we will be required to recognise our comfort zones. More than that, we will be required to move the boundaries out even further, in order to grow as human beings. Continuing the analogy above, we will have to move the tape out over an even wider zone, in order to make progress. I believe that incremental small steps, rather than gigantic leaps are the best way to extend our personal boundaries. Like gardening, the maxim for extending our comfort zones should be — little and often.
What does this look like in real life? Well, a few weeks ago I went to the local town to do some shopping. There are a limited number of car parks

and they were all full. I eventually ended up on a pay and display section of the local hotel. There was one space left. It became obvious why this space was empty when I got a little closer. It was a corner spot with tight access and two very solid brick walls for company. Tight. Very tight. If you managed to get in, then there was a fair chance that you would never get out. I stuck the car into reverse, resigned to driving off, and parking on the outskirts of town. Then suddenly, I thought — 'No'. It was time to challenge my parking comfort zone, and to give this a go. After about twenty-three manoeuvres, I eventually managed to get the car into the space.

Feeling very pleased with myself, I set off to do my shopping. About halfway around the shops, I suddenly developed a really uneasy feeling. OK, I had managed to park the car, but how on earth would I ever get it out of that space? For the rest of the shopping trip, I wrestled with thoughts of scraping the car along the brick walls, or hitting another car on the car park. By the time I got back to my car, I was almost a nervous wreck.

Before I started the engine, it occurred to me that I didn't have any options now. I had to get out of this space in order to drive home. Fifteen minutes and 103 movements later, I was driving off the car park unscathed. I couldn't believe it. I'd done it! I'd challenged my car parking comfort zones, and come out the other side. The feeling of satisfaction and elation was only matched by the incredible confidence and self–belief that poured over me in waves. Remarkable. It is probably true that if we do what we fear the most, then we control fear.

So what challenges are you currently shirking in your life at the moment? What tasks or situations are you avoiding and why? How would your life be if you faced up to one of your life challenges? What if you took on that impossible task, and came out on the other side unscathed? Easier said than done, I know. Because if you are anything like me, then there will be a little voice whispering in your ear, reminding you that you really don't have what it takes to do this. Remember all the previous attempts that ended in failure? Well you don't want to risk that again do you? Then there are all those big influences on your life so far. What would they have to say about what you are trying to do? Varying degrees of support and encouragement, I'll bet!

So who are, or have been, the most influential people in your life up to now? Take a moment to think about this one. The person that you are today, reflects everything that has happened to you in your life so far. The huge numbers of people with whom you have come into contact will also have influenced you, for better or for worse. All of these interactions will have made some impact upon you. As Dr Phil McGraw says, it's as if we are born with an 'empty slate', and people and events in our life will 'write on the slate', changing our life story.

Which events have left the greatest 'statements' on your slate? And why? Who are the people that have made the greatest impression on your slate? When I sat down to think about this, I was surprised as to whom I had allowed to be the real influencers in my life. I have a brother. He is three years older than me. For those of you who have older brothers or sisters, then you will probably be familiar with some of this stuff. We seemed to get along OK when we were young. However I can remember my first day at senior school. We had to catch a bus from Sutton to the other side of St Helens. Our house was a short walk to the bus stop. I can remember that awful feeling of nervous anxiety that we get as kids when we are faced with this kind of new situation. I can also remember my brother's friend calling for us, and rushing to catch up with them as they started off down the street. Imagine my shock and horror, when my brother turned around to me and told me in no uncertain terms, that, although he had been instructed to take me with him on my first day, there was no way that I was walking with them, and so had to follow on sheepishly a few steps behind. When the bus came, I had to sit on my own.

So what, I hear you cry? Well to a young kid, full of nerves and intrepidation, with a churning stomach and a new school blazer, the last thing you need is a lack of support and understanding! That day seemed to set the tone of my brother's attitude towards me for the next few years. He would always put me down, never give me a fair chance at anything, and ultimately became my number one enemy.

Now, you may have had something similar. The worst thing is that people like this, make you feel as if it is your fault. I can remember being told so many times by my brother that I was a useless idiot who would never amount to anything, that I began to believe it myself! I also believed that I must have done something terribly wrong to him, something so bad to deserve all this ill treatment. I have wracked my brains over and over to uncover the reason behind it all. Even now, with us both aged over 40, I still wonder what I must have done to upset him so badly?

Well, how about this? Maybe I didn't do anything wrong. Maybe he was the one with the problem. Yet I spent an awful lot of time growing up, dancing to his tune. Being the person that he dictated I should be. Meeting the expectations that he drew on my slate. So whose tune are you dancing to at the moment? And are you happy with it?

If you are, then fine. If not, then the good news is that you don't have to go a single day further with this slate. You have the power within you to take control of your body and soul, and wipe the slate clean now. There is nothing that we can do to change the past. Yet there is everything that we can do to mould the future. Resolve right here and now, today, to be true to yourself, to become the person you truly want to be, and to live your life in the way that you desire. Don't let anyone steal your dream…particularly family!

Accept the fact that you are who you are today because of everything that has happened to you in the past. All the choices and decisions that you have made, have brought you to exactly this point in your life. In fact, you could not be anywhere else. We will, however, be exploring a number of tools and techniques throughout the book, that will give you the confidence and belief that you can change things. The important thing is that it doesn't matter where you have been in the past; it is where you are going in the future that really matters. This really isn't a rehearsal. We only get one shot at life, so make a decision to live in the now, in the moment, and become your authentic self. The person you always wanted to be!

TAKING STOCK

Before we set about putting the world to rights, then it might be worth our while taking time to have a look at our own situation and see what changes, if any, need to be made. Given that you were sufficiently interested and curious to buy this book in the first place, then I'm going to make the assumption that you are not completely satisfied and happy with the way things are at the moment in your own particular universe? If this is not the case and you are as happy as a happy thing, then don't read any further. Take this book back to where you bought it and get a refund!

Just in the same way that people who are about to embark upon some sort of weight–loss programme tend to weigh themselves to get some idea of what their current position is, then I think it's vital that we do the same for our personal development plan. So how do we 'take stock' of our situation?

Well, a good starting point is to take a blank piece of paper and jot down all the various zones of your life that you want to examine. Zones that have come up in the past include — family life, finances, physical health, career, social life, and relationship with spouse/partner. The key thing here is that you choose the zones that are relevant to you.

Once you have chosen your life zones, draw yourself a bicycle wheel complete with a hub and spokes out to the tyre. The shape of the wheel is going to help us to make some sort of judgement as to where we see ourselves right now, in relation to each zone. The centre of the wheel, (the hub), will be rated zero, whilst the tyre at the outer edge of the wheel will carry a value of ten. The spoke that extends from the hub to the tyre can be marked off with the values of one to nine.

Now, this is where it gets interesting! Each of your life zones will go onto a different spoke of the wheel. Write in your life zone titles against a spoke. Once you have labelled up your wheel, then you can spend some time taking each zone in turn, and making a judgement as to how you would score it right now. So, for example, if physical health is one of your zones, then make a decision as to what score you would give yourself right now, with regards to your physical health? Are you in excellent health, eating a balanced and nutritious diet? Do you take regular and appropriate exercise?

Do you get enough quality rest? If so, then you may want to score yourself highly, say with a nine. Put a mark on your 'physical health' spoke, at the 'nine' point. On the other hand you may be out of condition, can't remember when you last took any exercise, eat whatever is in the cupboard and regularly feel as if you need another two hours sleep in a morning? If this rings bells with you, then you may score lower down the scale i.e. four or five.

One word of caution around finances or money. If you have this as a category, then don't be tempted to score it according to how much or how little money you have. Try instead to think about what your relationship is like with the money in your life at the moment. Are you content with your finances? Do you manage your money sensibly, spending wisely and saving enough to give you a degree of security if required? Or do you feel that they are out of control? Are you constantly going over–budget? Do you find yourself preoccupied with money, constantly thinking about how you are going to break even at the end of the month?

Once you have decided on your score for each zone, place a mark along the spoke of your wheel that corresponds to that particular life zone. Do this for all of your zones. You can then join up all of the marks to create an overall view of your life right now. Does your shape look like a perfect circle or is it more of a spider's web or a fried egg with some very high scores and some very low scores?

So what does this activity tell us? Well, if you have been honest with yourself, then it will give you an instant visual picture as to the way in which you feel about your life right now. There may be zones in your life that need more attention (and sooner) than others. Also you might want to think about how the zones affect one another. If you have some zones scoring very highly, then is that at the expense of other zones in your life, which are scoring particularly low? Would it be better to have a more balanced wheel whereby the scores were very similar, giving a smoother, rounder picture to your life?

Just take a moment to imagine what your life would be like if you were scoring a perfect ten in every zone. What would that look, feel and sound like? Is it feasible that you would ever get to a ten? Or is it perhaps more realistic to think that 9 is a more achievable score! Whatever your scores, is there any value whatsoever in having a really high score in one department of your life at the expense of another area? Which of the areas in your life are you neglecting at the moment and why? Would it be better to have lower scores that were more evenly balanced perhaps? What difference would this bring to our lives? As I write this book, the whole topic of work/life balance has become a major issue. In an ever–changing world following the incidents on September 11th, 2001, many people are examining their lives as never before. The Bicycle Wheel of Life will help us to do that, by giving us an instant visual as to how we view things at the moment. It's a subjective method, yet it's better than nothing, which is what the vast majority of people do.

Another thing to remember about this activity is that it will reflect a particular moment in your life. The wheel can and will change. Sometimes this will be as a result of external events and forces in our lives. Your job may be made redundant, and you may spend time between positions. This may impact upon several of your spokes, probably starting with your 'finance' zone! Conversely you may decide to take control of certain aspects of your life, plotting a path with clear and definite objectives that will fundamentally alter the way that you do things, which in turn will have a dramatic and positive effect on your wheel. You may decide to go self–employed, for example, and secure a lucrative contract that, once again, will change your wheel scores. The beauty of this exercise is that it involves a pen, some paper and a small amount of time. The wheel is not chiselled out on a marble plinth. It can and will change over time. Indeed I would suggest that your first attempt at producing your bicycle wheel of life should be followed very swiftly by your second effort. Give yourself a week between the two. See just how much of a difference this activity can make to the way you view your life, and the actions that it will prompt you to take, in order to bring about the changes that will make the greatest difference to the way you live. Future editions of your wheel may contain new zones. These will be the ones that are truly important to you. Also you will find that you become much more focussed on pushing up your lower scores, in order to create and achieve a feeling of balance. This in turn will prompt you to continue with your improvement plan as things suddenly start to fall into place, helping you to define and refine the life that you have always wanted to lead.

SUCCESS

In order to achieve 'success', we first have to define it in greater detail. Let's define it in our terms and not other peoples'. What does success mean to you? How will you know when you have been successful?

The best definition of 'success' that I have ever come across goes like this. Success is —

'The continuous accomplishment of planned objectives which are worthwhile to the individual.'

There are several things that make this definition so good. Let's look at the words used.

Continuous: This means that you keep on striving towards the achievement of your goals. And when one goal is achieved, then you sit down and work out your next set of goals. Like the poster says, success is a journey and not a destination.

Accomplishment: We need to keep going until our goal is achieved. If we are not making any progress whatsoever, then it's time to take stock of the situation and make sure that we are approaching the goal in the right direction. Success is the ability to go from failure to failure without losing our enthusiasm.

Planned: The work that you have put into your goal definition, means that you have an absolutely crystal clear vision of exactly what it is that you want to achieve and why, together with a plan for moving towards your goals. This is no ad hoc, back of an envelope strategy.

Objectives: We have a clear vision of what it is we are aiming to achieve.

Worthwhile: Worthwhile to whom? Worthwhile to you. If it isn't worthwhile to you, then why waste time in doing it? This is your life remember, so take it by the scruff of the neck.

The key thing is that this definition takes away the magic dust. Success is no longer the exclusive preserve of a bunch of people who happen to have made it onto our TV screens. Neither is success only related to the amount of money that we can manage to accumulate in our lives. Success becomes attainable for us all. Success becomes the small things in life, like managing to pay the mortgage for another month, or finding more time to spend with our families.

Success is failure turned inside out. What is it that is stopping you from claiming all of the successes that you deserve in your life right now? Resolve right now, to take control of your life by allowing yourself to be successful. We are truly as successful as we allow ourselves to be.

Many people fear success in the same way that they fear failure. In fact they will go out of their way to sabotage their successes in order to remain within the life parameters that they set for themselves. How many times have you done this? Come on, be honest with yourself. Think back to when all those opportunities came your way, and what was your initial response? I couldn't do that; it's not for me the wonderful new job, the fantastic house, an amazing life partner. I always remember a comment by a good friend of mine. We were talking about some really expensive luxury cars. I remember saying that we would never get the chance to own one. He turned to me and said — 'Well, they make these cars for someone to drive, so why shouldn't it be us?'

I think that this desire to sabotage success can be traced back to our earliest years and the pressures of our peer groups. Think back to your schooldays. Did you ever get full marks in a test at junior school? What happened? Were you carried out into the playground on the shoulders of your fellow classmates, as they celebrated your knowledge and intellect? Or were you the subject of a few sideways glances and did you end up playing hopscotch on your own? After a few ten out of tens, the reception may have turned a little nasty, to the point were you decided that maybe seven or eight was a better score, putting yourself firmly back in the pack of also–rans?

What is it about human nature that we can't abide to see people doing well and achieving success for themselves (however that success might be defined)? I believe it is due to the fact that the also–rans live in a world of mediocrity. This works well for them until anything happens to remind them that they are living in a world of mediocrity. Rather than take the time and make the effort to raise their levels and standards to the heights shown, they prefer instead the easier route of attempting to drag down the high–achiever to their levels. How many times has this happened to you? Worse still, how many times have you been guilty of being a member of the mediocre brigade? When was the last time you heard yourself giving 'advice' to your friends, colleagues, and family. Did you really have their best interests at heart? Or were you thinking more about yourself?

It is a fact that cream always rises to the top, in the same way that if you try to keep a beach ball held under water, then it will always force its way to the surface, no matter what. Don't spend a moment longer listening to or taking the 'advice' of all those well–meaning people in your life. Listen instead to your own instinct. You were born to succeed. It is only through the process of life that we become 'conditioned' to fail. Success is whatever and however you define it. So be bold and brave in your march towards setting and achieving everything that you want in your life. Remember, this really isn't a rehearsal.

And when you cross the finish line, or get the chequered flag, when you've achieved your goal…. remember to take time to celebrate your success. Be proud of your achievement. Realise, however that success is a journey, and the next level is waiting around the corner in your march towards being the best that you can be.

GOALS

If you are looking to bring about success in your life more by design than by accident, then goals will become very important to you.

I'm reminded of the story of Michael Schumacher, the Formula One racing driver. He had just been crowned as World Champion and was being interviewed for the umpteenth time, about his success. This particular interviewer asked a very banal question —

'Tell us, Michael, how did you get to become Formula One World Champion?'

Whether it was the champagne, or just his sense of humour, or the fact that he was tired and wanting to go home, I don't know. Schumacher's answer, however, certainly made me chuckle.

'Well,' he said, 'I was just out there driving around and then after a certain number of laps I noticed this bloke with a big chequered flag, and he was waving it madly up and down at me. The next thing I know, I'm on this podium thing and people are spraying champagne all over the place, and I've been given this big trophy and they are playing my national anthem!'

The reality, of course, is very different. Schumacher had a goal. To be the top driver in the world at the highest competitive level. He started out through the ranks of carting, before progressing through the lower formulas. He trained hard physically and mentally year after year. He prepared thoroughly with his team in order to achieve the fastest times that they possibly could. This preparation involved hundreds of practise laps and minor adjustments to the car. Following on from this was the intense effort required for each Grand Prix. The complete focus on achieving points. Until gradually those points began to add up to an unassailable lead. Before you knew it, success was one race away. Then…victory.

Moral of the story? Michael Schumacher had a goal. Not only that, he pursued his goal with a purpose and intention that ultimately secured him the prize.

Yet most people out there do not have any goals. Full stop. End of comment.

The vast majority of the population form part of what Zig Ziglar calls 'the wandering generality.' They go from day to day with little or no thought as to what it is they are doing or why they are doing it. Don't get me wrong. If you recognise yourself as part of this group, and you feel totally content and happy within yourself, then don't change. You may want to contact me (nhe@buzztalks.com) to get a full refund on this book, however, because it is my belief that goals are an integral part of achieving success.

A life without goals is a little bit like being in a rowing boat out at sea…without any means of navigation, and no oars! If you don't know where you are supposed to be going, then how will you know when you've got there?

What if you had a specific destination? What if you had all the navigational equipment necessary to help keep you on track? Maps, compass, a satellite phone and global positioning system? What if someone gave you a pair of huge oars to help you propel the boat in the right direction? What kind of a difference would that make to your journey? Goals make a huge difference. Setting goals will instantly take you from the 'wandering generality' and move you into the group of 'meaningful specifics'.

So how do we set goals? What is the secret? Well, what do you want to be, have and do with this life of yours? What are the burning desires that lurk in the darkest recesses of your soul? Whenever I have read about goal setting previously there is invariably a mention that all your goals should conform to the SMART method. This means that they should be —

Specific, Measurable, Achievable, Realistic and Time–bound

Whilst I agree in principal with this model, I think we have to be careful, particularly when deciding what is achievable and realistic. It is certainly true that there are going to be things that you will never achieve for a variety of reasons. If you are over forty, and over–weight, then it is very unlikely that you will be called up to play for the England first team at football, for example. What I would say, however, is that there are probably a whole range of things that are within our capabilities that we currently view as being unachievable. It is vital that we don't sell ourselves short when exploring the options and setting our goals.

Indeed in terms of realistic, I think there are certain activities and achievements that are definitely unrealistic to consider. The key issue with this is that, if we set unrealistic goals, then we are mentally defeated before we have even started. Our conscious mind will shut down and tell us that there is no chance of reaching the goal, so why bother in the first place. Much better to set goals and targets that are just beyond our comfort zone levels. Although this is quite scary, it is also very exciting, particularly when you achieve the goal and realise that you have taken a massive step in a new direction. Don't limit your thinking by setting goals that are too easy to achieve, or by setting goals that are far, far too challenging. By using this method you will stay motivated and committed to the self–development process, rather than defeated and deflated.

Break down your goals into stages. A simple method is to create a time–frame around long term, medium term and short term. This will give you milestones to achieve, and help you to maintain your motivation and momentum, especially when the going gets tough. It is possible to eat an elephant. You just have to take one bite at a time! So, if your ultimate aim is to run a marathon, for example, within the next twelve months, then you can work backwards from the long–term, setting yourself milestone targets for the process

Short term — (within the next month)
Target. Buy new kit — this week
Start eating more fresh fruit and veg / pasta — this week
Do three runs of two miles each — this week / month

Medium term (within six months from now)
Completing 4 runs per week of 5 miles each
Going to the gym twice a week for stamina sessions

Long term (within twelve months from now)
Completing four runs per week of 8 miles plus one long run of 15 miles
Going to the gym three times a week for stamina sessions

Remember that your goals are written down on paper and not chiselled out on a piece of rock. It is true, however, that a goal is not a goal unless it is written down. Anyone can carry around a head full of wishful thinking. Have the courage to commit your goals to paper. You can change your goals and adapt them as your circumstances change. In reality, the important thing is not the goals themselves, (although they will have value to you) but the actual process of goal setting. This will give you the purpose, drive and the motivation to take action to move towards the accomplishment of your goals.

Once you have your goals defined, take a moment to review them. Do they meet the SMART criteria? Do they excite you so much that you want to get started on them straight away? Think carefully as well, about the people who are going to help you to achieve your goals. Very often people, who are 'fresh' to the goal–making procedures, rush off and wave their newfound direction under everyone else's nose. Be warned. In the majority of cases you will only succeed in getting up those very same noses.

Before you run around like a mad thing, have another look at your goals. They will generally fall into two distinct categories. These are 'give up' and 'get up'.
A 'give up' goal may be something like — 'I want to give up smoking' for example. A 'get up' goal might be — ' I want to double my income in the next two years'.

Feel free to share your 'give up' goals with as many people as you like, provided that you know they will work with you in your attempts to bring the goal to fruition. Conversely, do not share your 'go up' goals with anyone, unless you can absolutely guarantee that they are 100% behind you. Otherwise you may just be inviting sabotage into the camp. After all, people don't like to feel that they are being left behind. They won't want you rocking the boat. That would only expose their shortcomings.

So, you've got your goals all written down. You've got your support team in place. You can always make a start on them tomorrow can't you? Because Eastenders is on TV tonight and then that other programme that looks really interesting. Well, watching TV is all well and good if the programme is genuinely educational or entertaining. Yet how many of us fritter away our lives just watching other people live theirs? The programme 'Big Brother' is the ultimate realisation of this.

Your goals will not become reality if you waste your precious time staring blankly at the box in the corner. Remember that everything you do will either move you towards, or take you away from your goals. Spend your time wisely. It is after all, your most valuable resource. And remember, the journey of 1,000 miles really does start with the first step.

AFFIRMATIONS

I am not a psychologist, nor am I a psychiatrist. So I would like to hear from those of you who are, in order that you could explain to me the workings of the subconscious mind. (Please feel free to email me — nhe@buzztalks.com) There are lots of simplistic diagrams, which draw the analogy between the conscious and subconscious minds and an iceberg. The theory is that the conscious mind represents only the tip of the iceberg, whereas the subconscious is made up of the larger mass, which floats unseen under the water.

The subconscious mind is therefore a crucial part of our existence. Yet how much time and effort do we devote to it? What if we could get this huge amount of untapped potential to work for us, rather than simply lying dormant?

How many times have you gone to bed worrying over an issue only to wake up the next morning with a ready made solution? Then there is the time–honoured expression — 'I'll sleep on it?' It would appear that the subconscious mind is active even when we are asleep. It has also been suggested that the subconscious mind cannot tell the difference between what is real and what is imagined. If I started to talk about a really hot summer's day, for example, and then described in great detail how you might pour a long cool drink of sparkling water, I would guarantee that most of us would 'see' the glass in our mind's eye. We would 'hear' the carbonated bubbles fizzing and popping as they rose from the bottom of the glass and burst out through the surface. What if I then suggested that we add a couple of ice–cubes? We all know the chinking sound that they make as they hit the sides of the glass, which suddenly becomes cool to the touch. Suppose we then decide to add a slice of lemon? Feel the waxy rind of the lemon as you slice it open with your sharpest knife. The juice runs over your fingers as you pick up one half. You raise it up to your mouth, and take a huge bite of this sweet smelling citrus fruit…

So how many of you have suddenly found yourself salivating?

Yet all that I described there was just a figment of my imagination. It's amazing how the mind can play 'tricks' upon us, creating a real physical response to something that was just imagined. What if we could harness that power to work for us, supporting our efforts to achieve success, rather than sabotaging them? Because we do sabotage our efforts, don't we?

Most of us talk to ourselves. It's a little bit like having a monkey on your shoulder, constantly chattering away in your ear. And what does the monkey tell us? What is the content of this self–talk? Well, I would suggest that most of the time it is of a negative nature, giving us reasons why we can't, won't, or shouldn't do something. Am I right? It's a bit like gardening. If you leave a garden to its own devices, then it will eventually sprout weeds. It's the same with our self–talk. If we don't actively take control of it, then it will automatically switch to the negative.

So what can we do? What is the mental equivalent of weeding the garden?

I believe that the answer lies in the use of affirmations. These are positive, statements, which allow us to say 'yes' to our potential. An example of an affirmation might be — 'I have all the money I need for my life right now.'

In order for affirmations to be successful, it is crucial that they are written following the 'three P' rule. They need to be personal to us. In order to achieve this, they should be written using the first person — 'I'. Affirmations should also be written in the present tense, as if the situation that you desire has already been achieved. This seems to inspire the subconscious mind to come up with ways of bringing the situation described in the affirmation, into reality. Remember, we said that the subconscious mind couldn't tell the difference between what is real, and what is imagined. A good way of creating the present tense with your affirmations is to add the word 'now' at the end of the statement. An example of this might be — 'I am in excellent health now.' Writing affirmations in the present tense helps to create a mental picture of your life, as you would like it to be. It is surprising how, once you have written your affirmations, you suddenly start to become the person that you always wanted to be, how opportunities suddenly seem to open up for you, and how you start to rapidly move towards the achievement of your goals. The final 'P' in the affirmation equation is the need to state your desires and intentions in a positive manner, rather than a negative one. Why?

Well the subconscious mind seems to respond better to statements written in this way. So, if one of your affirmations was a statement designed to help you become a non–smoker, for example, you may be tempted to write — 'I don't smoke cigarettes anymore'. At first glance, this might look OK, and indeed it may serve as some sort of reminder to you to try NOT to do something. However, if we then compare the statement — 'I am a non–smoker now'.
We can see how much more powerful the affirmation becomes for being written with a positive slant.

So now we can spend some time writing our affirmations. Remember to think about all areas of your life in order to create a comprehensive and complete set of life–enhancing statements. Remember also the key principles —

Personal, present tense and positive

What do I do with my affirmations?
So you've spent some time writing your statements out? Easy wasn't it? What do you mean 'No?' Well actually I agree with you on that one. Writing your affirmations, if it is done properly and with a degree of contemplation, may well take you some considerable time. After all it's not every day that you get to create a blueprint for your future is it? However, let's assume that you now have a comprehensive and well–crafted set of statements. And you did write them out didn't you? Remember in the same way that a goal is not a goal unless it is written down, then an affirmation remains nothing more than a thought in your mind. Get your affirmations written down, preferably typed out. You may want to put them in a protective plastic wallet. Why? Because they will form the basis for your guiding map, just like as if you were going orienteering. Just like an orienteering map, we are going to be referring to them on a regular basis

and so it makes sense to protect it before it gets all dog–eared and coffee–stained! It is my personal belief that, in the early days, it makes sense to carry them with you at all times. I would certainly suggest that you refer to them as soon as you are fully awake. Start the day the affirmation way. Even if this means setting the alarm just that little bit earlier, allow yourself the opportunity to read through your statements without interruption. Easier said than done, I know. However if you are truly serious about making changes in your life in order to become the person that you've always wanted to be, then expect a few challenges along the way. After all, if it was so easy and required little or no effort on your behalf, then you would have done it years ago, right? If you carry your affirmations with you, then you can enjoy them at any time throughout the day. Allow yourself the opportunity to refresh mentally yourself, and maintain your focus. This is especially true when you will be faced with the many challenges that we will all inevitably face as we go through our daily business.

If you do nothing else, however, then I would suggest it is crucial to scan your affirmations through last thing at night just before you go to sleep. Repeat the statements either out loud or in your head, over and over until they become second nature. This process will help to embed them into your subconscious mind. It can then go to work for your helping to create the circumstances, situations and solutions to bring the statements into reality.

A few final points on affirmations. They are not carved in stone. You can add to them as you achieve your successes and replace outdated statements. Also be very careful about sharing your affirmations with anyone, unless you know that they will be supportive towards the concept. Most people will find the concept of 'positive self-talk' either complete lunacy or slightly scary. Remember that you are doing this for you in order to achieve your dreams and goals. In these circumstances, all exposure to potential negative and energy sapping sources should be limited and kept to an absolute minimum.

Perhaps the most important point regarding affirmations is to realise that whilst they are a tool to enhance your state of mind into accepting and becoming the person that you want to be, on their own they remain merely a set of nice statements. It is vital that you appreciate the need to take actions to move towards bringing the statements one step closer to reality.

Remember — life rewards action. Everything else is just conversation.

MONEY

The actor Jim Carrey was giving a TV interview and the topic of conversation came around to the meaning of success. The interviewer suggested to Jim that some of the films he had appeared in had been 'unsuccessful' due to the amount of money that they had made at the box office.

Jim Carrey replied with obvious feeling, that the concept of success, in his opinion, had absolutely nothing to do with money. Whilst the amount of money taken at the box office was one measure of how the film had done, Jim had a whole host of other factors that he used to 'measure' his performance.

For so many of us, the concept of success is becoming inextricably linked to money, so that the more you accumulate, then the more successful you are. This is a myth that is constantly perpetuated by the media, with the current obsession with so–called 'celebrities'.

Don't misunderstand me. I don't have a problem with the accumulation of wealth. In fact I see it as a natural by–product of the provision of a useful service. I do think, however, that we need to re–dress the balance at least in our own minds, with regards to what money means to us, and how we manage our relationship with it. We also need to recognise that the accumulation of money is by no means the only way to measure success in our lives.

Money, however, is an important feature in our lives. By the way, it is the love of money that is the root of all evil, not money itself. We all need it to get by don't we? Yet everyone's circumstances are different. We all view amounts of money differently. For some people £500,000 would be a substantial amount, for others it would represent a week's shopping money! It's not so much the amount of money that matters, more the relationship that you have with and towards the money in your life.

If the accumulation of great wealth is one of our goals, then we need to adopt a more strategic and controlled approach to attracting money. Given that the odds imply you are more likely to be struck by chemical waste from an airplane than win the lottery jackpot, simply picking six numbers out every week, does not guarantee success.

So. What do we want to achieve in our lives with regards to money? You may want to refer back at this point, to your Bicycle Wheel of Life, and identify what your current relationship is like with the cash in your life. The important thing here is to remember that money is like a mountain stream. It has a direction of flow. Money will therefore flow into our lives and will flow out of our lives. This concept of 'flow' is true for absolutely everyone. Even the most destitute of persons, living rough on the streets will have a 'flow', albeit drastically reduced from most of society. That is, at some point, someone will come along and give them a donation. Even if the donation is 10p or €1, then it still constitutes flow.

Yet what is our natural instinct once money has 'flowed' into our lives? Yes, that's right, we clasp our hands tightly around it, and try to hold on to it for dear life, don't we? Or you may belong to the alternative school that regards being in possession of money like being left holding the parcel when the music stops. You need to ship it on, i.e. spend it as soon and as quickly as possible!

Once you have got used to the idea that money literally 'flows' through your life, you can then start to build a relationship with your money. You can begin to have some fun as you learn to release your money with joy. This is particularly satisfying when you have to deal with what I call the 'grudge' spends in your life.

What qualifies as a 'grudge' spend? Well for me, these are all those bills and outgoings that have to be met, yet for which you don't get either much recognition or overt satisfaction. I'm really thinking in terms of stuff like the various utility bills, phone bills, council tax, etc etc. If you're anything like me you 'begrudge' paying these because there really isn't anything very exciting or satisfying about them. I mean, what do you get for your money???

Here is one way of changing your attitude and relationship to your grudge spends. This great idea comes from Jack Black. In order for this to work, it is necessary to write a cheque, (so if you have all your payments on a direct debit, you may want to think about adding a narrative if you can). When the payment is due, simply take your cheque and, at the very top, above the line with the instruction to 'pay', write in block capitals —
'With joy and pleasure'
Fill out the rest of the cheque details as per normal. Once you have done this, then turn the cheque over, and on the back write —

'This amount goes out into the world and enriches it, before coming back to me multiplied.'

You can then sign your name underneath.

They can't touch you for it, yet you will be amazed at how differently this simple act makes you feel towards your 'flow'. It really helps to release your money with a much more positive attitude, knowing that it will come bouncing back with interest! I have been doing this now for several years and I can safely say that it has the most impact when money is at its tightest!

So how much money do you need? How much money do you want? It is important to get serious about these figures if we want to create measurable financial goals. Everyone's answers will be different. Yet the crucial factor is that if you want to improve your financial reserves, then you first of all need to get serious about exactly how much. This will help to trigger the goal–setting process which in turn will help you to focus on the short term activity that you may need to undertake in order to accomplish your planned objective.

You may want to get a better–paid job, for example, or even change careers to something more lucrative than the occupation you are currently engaged in. Or you might simply want to save more and spend less. Whatever it is, you can then start to break down your objectives into immediate action points.

What will you need to do, if you are to change jobs? Probably the first thing will be to get serious about what it is that you want. Will it involve relocation? Will you have to undertake some training in order to raise your knowledge and skills levels? What about your CV. Have you got one? Is it up to date and appropriate? As well as goal setting around your objectives, it is vital that you remember to affirm your success. This will require spending time visualising the outcome, then writing up those present tense, personal, positive statements that describe you as if you had already achieved your goal. Drawing up your affirmations, and referring to them at least twice daily, will set in motion the thought processes that will drive you towards taking action. Remember, we become what we think about. So, if you find your relationship with money is currently challenged, you might want to adopt the affirmation —

'My personal and business finances are in perfect order, now'.

You will be amazed by the calmness that will overcome all your financial dealings, once you accept this as true for your life. Opportunities to generate and receive money will suddenly appear in your everyday world.

Get serious today about your finances. Work out what you want and how you are going to get there. Then start right now to make the changes in your life that will move you towards your financial goals. Examine every aspect of your financial life. Are you paying too much for things? Do you spend money unnecessarily by way of habit? Making small savings in your current lifestyle will have a bigger impact than you could imagine. It really is true that if you look after the pennies then the pounds will look after themselves.

Remember that money itself is worthless. It is just a collection of coins and paper. It's what we do with the money that gives it its value. So examine and accept the flow of money in your life. Learn to release it with joy. Spend it wisely and effectively. Give some away to a worthy cause if you want you. You'll be amazed at how this will make you feel. It really is better to give than to receive. And remember that there are no pockets in shrouds. ……..

POSITIVE ACTION

Years ago I remember someone finishing a presentation about personal development. They lit a candle and placed it in front of the group. They then suggested that we all focus our minds on the flame of the candle and use the power of thought to make it go out. I can remember the strong silence of the concentration as we all mentally urged this flame to die down….
Of course it did nothing of the sort, until the presenter threw a glass of water over it! The point he was trying to make was that thought processes on their own are generally not enough. If you want something to happen then you have to take action.

This is where many people fall down. They spend time and effort identifying their life zones, writing out goals and affirmations…. And then sit back waiting for the good times to roll. Well, I've got news for you. It doesn't happen like that. I love the old Chinese proverb —

'Person who stands on side of mountain waiting for roast duck to fly in…got long wait.'

In other words — life rewards action. Yes, you have taken massive steps towards improving things in your life by undertaking the exercises in this book. However on their own, they are not enough. The most important thing that you can do now, today, is to take action towards your goals. Every single thing that you do either moves you towards or takes you away from your goals. Every single thing.

The most effective way to ensure that you follow this maxim, and the most practical of all the tips and techniques that successful people use to stay focussed is to write a 'to do' list. It really is amazing that the simple act of spending a few moments writing down what you want to achieve that day, will do more for your march towards achieving your goals, than any amount of motivational reading material. Why is this so effective?

Well, the human brain is the most amazing thing. It's probably still true today that we are way off knowing the full story as to how it works. The complexity and richness of its structure and functionality will keep the research scientists going for ages yet! One thing that we do know, however, is that we are way off using the brain to anywhere near its capacity. Why is it, for example, when you go shopping because you need certain items, you invariably come back with a bag full of groceries, and forget to buy the one item that you set out with the intention of getting? Why is it that we forget someone's name almost in the same instant that we are introduced to them?

We don't appear to have mastered the art of remembering things at all well. In fact, I read somewhere recently that the average person is capable of remembering only seven things (+ or − 2). In reality what that creates is a sense of chaos in our lives whereby we are constantly playing 'catch–up', rushing around without any structure or purpose to our activities. We are reactive rather than proactive.

By taking a few moments to jot down all the events, factors and tasks that you need to consider in your day, you are giving yourself the advantage of a mental safety net. You will no longer need to juggle with your memory, since all the important stuff is written down in front of you. You can simply take out your list and refer to it.

Once you have your list, you can then start to order the items in accordance with your priorities. The important and urgent stuff should take priority over the unimportant and non–urgent activities in your life. Something will be important if doing it has a high benefit, and it will be urgent if there is a point in time whereby if it is not done, then the benefit of doing it is cancelled or significantly reduced. Once you have prioritised your list, then you can set about completing the activities. This is where the fun starts. Why? Because you know that you are striving to live your life in an effective way. Plus you get to cross off the tasks on your list once they are completed. This will give you a tremendous sense of achievement and well–being, which creates and maintains the momentum to continue working towards your goals.

Just a couple of quick tips on the 'to do' list. Don't worry if you don't get to cross everything off in one day. It happens. Simply start the next day's list by transferring your uncompleted activities over. If you keep ending up with the same things left undone, then you might want to ask yourself the questions —

Is this activity important to me?
Am I avoiding tackling this job for some reason?

I would also suggest that you do your 'to–do' list at the same time every day. Why? Well it creates a positive habit pattern. Good habits take a little bit of effort. They are hard to form, yet very easy to live with. Conversely, bad habits are easy to form, yet hard to live with. It doesn't matter what time of day you do your list, just as long as it becomes a habit.

You might want to think about breaking the tasks down into their component parts. So, for example, on my list I might have put — 'write a book'. What happens is that this task is a big one, and there are lots of things that need to happen, before I get to cross it off. There is a fair chance that simply transferring this task over and over onto my daily list might disillusion me. So instead, why not break the whole task down into smaller, more readily achievable tasks, such as 'write 500 words for Chapter 1'. This is much more instantly achievable, thereby allowing me to cross something off my list. In this way the momentum is maintained rather than destroyed.

By remaining focussed on the short–term things that you can do, you will find that they eventually become giant strides towards achieving everything that you desire. It really is a cliché, however the journey of a thousand miles starts with the first step. Know as well, that the journey will present challenges. How often do things go completely smoothly? Yes, there may be setbacks, yes, you will hit friction and resistance, and yes, people will become jealous of your progress and try to sabotage your success. Be ready for it; accept it as part of the procedure. However don't let it alter your determination to see this journey through. You've made a commitment to yourself to be the best that you can be. Don't let anyone steal your dreams.

DEALING WITH RESISTANCE

So you've set your goals, you've written you affirmations, and you've started to take action every day to move you towards the achievement of success in every area of your life? In fact almost overnight you've become this zealous convert to the cause of motivation and self–improvement.

And what happens?

Well you start to get strange looks from people. Your new–found energy and enthusiasm appears to cause concern, particularly amongst your family, friends and work colleagues. Relax. This is entirely normal. Remember that they probably haven't read this book yet, so they have some ground to catch up! Plus there is a huge wave of negativity in the UK, which carries the wandering generality along in its path. The media perpetuates this wave. For some bizarre reason we seemed to be trapped in a spiral of only reporting negative news. Listen to the news tonight and make a list of the stories as they come up. Make a judgement as to whether or not you thought the item was positive or negative. Now I'm not saying that we should all deny reality. However, given the choice, would you rather expose yourself to information that uplifts your very being and inspires you to work towards your goals? Or would you rather wallow in a mire of negative stuff that drags your heart down to your toes?

The choice is yours. Make a vow not to expose yourself unnecessarily to any negative source in the media. Resolve here and now, not to watch the TV news or buy a newspaper for the next 21 days. See what a difference it will make to your attitude. Don't worry. If there is a news story that you really need to be aware of, then it will come to you!

Another factor to remember is that your newfound direction and purpose will, inevitably make people feel slightly uncomfortable. Why? Because your sense of drive and focus will encourage them to look at their own lives and realise that they are doing nothing to improve and move forward. Their natural reaction in this circumstance won't be to spend time working on their strategy for success. No, that looks too much like hard work!

The easier option is to make sure that you don't make any progress towards your goals, so that you don't embarrass them any further. They may begin to adopt childish tactics in order to keep you in your place. It's a little bit like the school thing again. Remember when you were a kid at school and you used to get ten out of ten in the spelling tests? After a while you realised that everyone else was getting fives and sixes, and they didn't much like the fact that you were such a smarty–pants. So, what did you do? Well it's easy enough to sabotage the odd answer so that you could slip back into the relative obscurity of mediocrity, wasn't it? That may have been a strategy that worked in infant school. Is it really something that we should be using in our adult lives? How many times have you sabotaged yourself lately in order to fall in line with the pack?

The comedian Harry Enfield can take some of the blame. He created a character whose catchphrase went something like …

'You don't want to be doing that.'

This champion of negativity is not exclusive to the Harry Enfield show. He or she will pop up with alarming regularity in your life. Listen out for them as they spread their doom and gloom throughout the land. These people will attempt to suck your energy dry. They are generally unable to view the positive side to any situation and will be aghast at your drive and determination. They will go to great lengths to drag you down their negative alley, they may even laugh at you.

So who are they? Only you will know. Spend some time thinking about all the people in your life at the moment. If you had to label them as either positive or negative, then who would be in either list? How can you reduce or eliminate your contact with the negative influences in your life? Remember that birds of a feather flock together. As you begin to practice the strategies in this book and achieve more and more success in your life, then you will find that you will attract more and more people with the same mindset and approach to life as yourself. You will no longer be able to tolerate the negativity and resistance that previously was a daily part of your routine.

This is a natural process and you should not be concerned if you find yourself looking to make serious changes in your life as a consequence of the need and desire to reduce or remove the negative influences in your life.

As it is always better to prevent rather than cure, then analyse your sources of negativity. You may have the luxury of being able to remove them from your equation of life. But what about the constant sources, the ones that we come into contact with everyday, friends, family and work colleagues who may fall into this category? Regular exposure to negative influences will easily undo all your hard work in creating positive change in your life....if you allow it to. Just as in the same way that no one can make you feel inferior without your consent, then you have ultimate control over how these negative influences will affect you, don't you?

Keep reading your affirmations. Be assertive and tell the offenders that you believe they have a negative approach to issues and that you do not share their opinion. Ask them the question, "Why do you appear to have such a negative slant on life?" You can also have fun with the Buzz Lightyear approach. You may remember him from the film Toy Story; He spends most of it with his helmet visor down to protect him from the potentially toxic air of the unfamiliar planet that he finds himself on. Well, what if we had an imaginary helmet that we could bring down whenever we wanted to? As soon as we detect negativity we could close off the potentially toxic attitudes, and breath deeply in our own purified, positive affirmations.

Again, let me stress, I'm not saying that we should deny reality, however we should take a more proactive approach to the information and attitudes that we choose to absorb. After all you wouldn't put mud in the petrol tank of your car would you? So why allow the mental equivalent of mud into your mind? Take control of your body and soul. We may not have a choice about some things in life, however we do have ultimate control over our attitude. How we view and interpret events is completely down to use. The glass is either half full or half empty. It's down to us which view we take.

It's a bit like the weather forecast. How many times have you heard the forecasters say that we are in for a spell of unpleasant weather? Well who decides that it is unpleasant? I love the quote that says —

'There is no such thing as bad weather, only the wrong clothes.'

Our attitude is just about the only thing that we can control in this crazy world. Make a resolve today to adopt a more positive attitude to everything. After all attitudes are contagious. The question you have to ask yourself is, —

Is mine worth catching?

BELIEF

Do you believe that you can do it? I mean really believe that you can? Because without unshakeable self–belief, then all the goal–setting, affirming and the taking of positive action will be worthless if, deep down inside, you really don't believe that you will achieve your aims. We've all seen them haven't we? We've all met one, or know of one. The people who, in their heart of hearts, really didn't think that it was going to happen anyway. Oh yes, they tagged along for the ride and made all the right noises. However when the walls came tumbling down, they could be heard bleating things like, 'Course, I knew it wasn't going to work really.'

It never ceases to amaze me when top sportsmen and women are being interviewed prior to a major event. The interviewer will invariably ask them who they think will win. I can't remember the number of times I've sat in astonishment as they begin to reel off a number of their direct competition. What?? You're asking me who is going to win? Well, I'm going to win. That's why I'm here, that's what I've been training for all of these months. This is my goal and I'm going to achieve it. Come what may.

Are you equal to the best that there is? Of course you are. Possibilities are that you are even better than the best there is. If only you would give yourself a chance. Just one. We are all as successful as we allow ourselves to be. It's amazing, isn't it, how that concept of self–belief, what you ultimately believe about yourself, will shine through regardless. After all, how many times have you said to yourself, 'I'll never get that dream job, that new car, a place in the first team, my ultimate life partner.' How many times have things gone well for you? So well that you have had to sabotage your success and snatch defeat from the jaws of victory? Why, because ultimately you believe, for whatever reason, that you don't deserve all of these good things in life.

So what is your excuse? Your background, upbringing, family, friends, parents? What? Why do you continue to behave in a way that denies you the opportunity to become the person that you really want to be, and believe yourself to be? It took me quite a while to understand that all the derogatory things that my brother said to, and about me, whilst we were growing up, were not actually true. People will try a whole host of things to make their candle appear to shine more brightly than yours. One trick is to attempt to blow your candle out.

The time has come. Resolve now to stand up and be counted. After all if you won't stand up for what you believe in, then you'll sit down for anything. Don't let another day go by where you allow someone to either say or do something that you do not feel comfortable with. Life really is too short to listen to the nonsense that other people produce, simply because we appear as a threat to them in some way.

There is only one person who has the right to dictate your levels of self-belief, and that's YOU. Yes, I said YOU. Just in the same way that no one can make you feel inferior without your consent, then you have ultimate control over your levels of self-belief. It really is all down to you. It's also down to you to challenge and build your levels of confidence and self-belief, as you move towards becoming the real you. The authentic you.

So how do we do it then? How do we achieve unshakeable self-belief? Well, if you have already started to put some work into your affirmations, then you will already be seeing a real difference in the way that you feel about things in general. Your affirmative statements will give you a well–formed idea of 'success' across all aspects of your life. Of course simply repeating your affirmations in themselves is not the whole story. Unshakeable confidence and self–belief are also built up as you challenge yourself to achieve more in all aspects of what you do. Remember that every single action of every single day either takes you towards or moves you away from your goals. So, in the same way every small success that you achieve is like adding another brick in the wall of your self–belief. The more bricks that you add, then the higher the wall gets.

Listen out to the language that is used around you. Cynicism and sarcasm are not going to assist you in your march towards your goals. I'm not saying that we should ignore reality, however unshakeable self–belief is based on confident optimism rather than negative pessimism. Challenge yourself to raise the bar in everything that you do. Take small yet incremental steps towards creating the life that you desire and deserve. Know that it lies out there waiting for you. Believe it can be.

DESIRE

How badly do you want it? Are you really serious about putting the effort in to achieve your goals? How long will it be before you decide that the effort needed to change is greater than you imagined and that it will be easier to stay the same?

What excuses will you offer to yourself, your friends, family, work colleagues, when you fall off the wagon? We've become a nation of easy–lifers, haven't we? We want it all, with cream on top, yet we are not prepared to put in the effort nor make the sacrifices necessary to achieve real and lasting success in our lives. We've all done it. Made those New Year resolutions that become vacant, empty, idle threats and promises by the first week in February. Oh yes, we start off with the good intentions, the gym membership, the no–smoking campaign, the first week of self–discipline. Then it all goes pear–shaped. Why is this?

Well, there are two things happening here. Firstly, we are not serious about making the changes that we need to. When we make a decision to do something, then we should look at the Latin roots of the verb that we are using. It breaks down into two parts — 'de' which means from and 'caedere' which means 'to cut'. So the literal translation of the verb is to 'cut from'. When we make a decision, we should see it as cutting away from the old habit pattern, and choosing a different one. No 'ifs', no 'buts'. Once you make a decision, you stick to it, no matter what. People say giving up smoking is one of the most difficult things to do. Well, I disagree entirely. It's not a question of will power or determination. Nor is it anything to do with physical cravings. It's more mental strength. Remember, if you want to, then you will. Set goals in a different direction. One that does not allow for the habit of smoking.

I remember the time when I smoked. My partner and I had just bought our first house together, and we sat down to work out the finances of how we were going to be able to afford it. Up until that point I had never really thought about the consequences of my smoking. It was just something that I did. When we worked out our financial outgoings, I was absolutely amazed to discover that I was spending about the same amount a month on cigarettes, as I was required to put up for my share of the mortgage. That was enough incentive right there to convince me that I had to make a decision to stop. Get yourself a compelling enough reason, and you can change any habit pattern that you want.

The second major reason why we fall by the wayside when making life–changing decisions is all to do with motivation. Actually it is more to do with the lack of motivation, or more accurately, the fall–off in motivation.

You know how it goes. You start on something new, and you're full of enthusiasm. In fact you're probably overflowing with it. You buy all the latest kit, and go overboard with the activity. Then as the enthusiasm wanes, and the momentum of your motivation starts to slow down, all of a sudden there are so many essential TV programmes to be watched, and two cars to be washed. You know when you've reached the critical moment when the indoor cycle fitness machine suddenly transforms into a useful thing to hang your clothes on. Our motivation declines. Pure and simple. It's really very easy to get motivated in the first place. The trick is to keep yourself motivated, especially when faced with the draining, mundane realities of everyday life.

So what can we do to combat this terminal condition? Keep focussed on your goal. Surround yourself with images of what it is that you are working to achieve. Build rewards into your plan so that each level of success, no matter how slight, is acknowledged and celebrated accordingly. Remember that everything you do either moves you towards, or takes you away from your goal. Don't be too hard on yourself. Remember that your goals and targets should be just far enough out there to make you feel slightly scared, however not too far out of reach so that you shut down straight away. You are capable of great achievements, far more than you have produced so far in your life. Let's face it, you've got where you are today without really pushing yourself too hard. What might you achieve if you truly harness your efforts and energies towards completely well formed outcomes?

Tell the people who matter, what you are attempting to achieve. The fact that you have shared your objectives with others will make it far more difficult for you to cave in so readily when the going gets tough. After all, you really don't want all that — 'I knew he/ she would never do it', stuff, do you?

Finally, believe. Truly believe in yourself and your abilities. Despite all your own best attempts to sabotage your successes in the past, together with the utter nonsense that you have had to put up with from others, recognise that now is the time. In the words of Sergei Bubka — 'If not you then who? If not now then when?' Don't allow another day to go by where you surrender your ultimate power of destiny to others. It is true that we either create the future of our choice, or we live out someone else's creation. Which is it to be?

MOMENTUM

My granddad used to have a small plot of land. He kept a few chickens and grew some vegetables. Nothing fancy. When we were very small kids, he used to take my brother and me to the plot…pushing us both in his wheelbarrow! At the end of the allotment, was the railway line. Occasionally we would go down and watch the trains. One particular day, a train had stopped just by granddad's fence, so we tootled down to have a look. I can vividly remember standing by the side of this huge black, oily, hissing, clanking, smoking, dripping thing. (This was back in the days of steam trains). It seemed enormous. There where two huge wheels on the engine that were joined together by a big metal bar. I remember being in complete awe at the size and weight of this magnificent piece of engineering.

I also remember being totally confused as to how the thing moved. As it stood there, stock still, groaning and creaking away, it occurred to me that it was just too heavy and bulky to propel itself, and that the trains that we had seen speeding by at full tilt through the countryside, must have been made from a different, more lightweight material? This lump was going nowhere.

Just at that moment, there was a loud blast on the hooter, and the wheels began to slowly creak forward. As they did, the whole train suddenly stretched and clanked as the connecting chains between the different cars tightened and took the strain. There was a loud hissing of steam, which suddenly began to escape from all parts of the engine. The connecting bar on the two front wheels slowly began to move in a strange elliptical way, as this mass of iron began to roll forward. The whole train started to slowly chug, chug, and chug as a rhythm of movement gradually developed. With each chugging heave, a huge plume of smoke would escape out from a tall chimneystack on top of the engine car.

Slowly but surely, the train started to gather speed, and this created a momentum, which built up until the whole thing was moving at great pace. It was funny because I remember looking at the train when it was

stationary, thinking —
'They'll never get this thing started!'
As we stood there, sucking on steam, with the train rapidly becoming a
black dot on the horizon, I suddenly thought —
'They'll never get it stopped!'
Momentum.

In science, momentum is a clearly defined concept. It exists and can be
measured very accurately by the equation —

$$MOMENTUM = MASS \times VELOCITY$$

In life I think we could say that this formula can be adjusted to —

$$MOMENTUM = COMMITMENT \times ENTHUSIASM$$

So what momentum do you have in your life right now? The tricky thing
with momentum, as we saw with the train, is that it takes lots more energy
to get movement into something that is stood stock-still. It is harder to get
something rolling from a standing start. The other side of the coin,
however, is that it is much easier, and takes far less effort, to keep an object
going, once it is moving. This is due to its momentum.

It is also a fact that, if we let an object come to rest again, after a period of
movement, then it will take more energy and effort to get it re–started on
its path, than if we had kept it moving in the first place. So what are the
lessons for us? Well, we need to make a start at creating and maintaining
momentum in our lives. The first stage to achieving this is to set goals.
Once we have done this and are sure of our intended direction, then we
need to make a commitment to take action towards those goals every day.
Life rewards action. Resolve to do something every single day, that moves
you towards, and not away from your goals. Each step that you take forward
helps to create and build momentum in your life.

There are things that slow down that momentum though aren't there? Life
sometimes gets in the way of action doesn't it? After all, there are so many

great programmes on TV. You may encounter setbacks along the way, when things do not go according to plan. There may be a degree of resistance applying an opposite force to your forward motion. Well, tell me honestly, have you ever seen anything run perfectly smoothly in any of your 'life' projects so far? No. It doesn't happen. Things break, don't work, and go wrong. People promise the earth and then don't even show up. If you get in the car and decide to go somewhere, then I can guarantee that, if you keep going long enough, you will hit a set of traffic lights. I can also guarantee that at some stage on your journey, those lights will be on red! Setbacks are inevitable, however don't let the friction and resistance of everyday people and everyday life take away your commitment to yourself to work towards, and keep working towards your goals.

Stick at the task, no matter what. Rest, by all means, however be mindful of the fact that you risk losing your momentum, and all that that entails, if you take your eye off the ball for too long. The amazing thing is that once you begin to create momentum in your life, by continually taking action towards your goals, you begin to feel differently about things. Obstacles suddenly become stepping–stones. You begin to attract people and opportunities into your life that you would otherwise have thought impossible. Success really does breed success, and as you keep making small achievements on your path to your ultimate goals, your momentum will take on a life of its own, fuelling you with the confidence and abilities to pursue and achieve things beyond even your wildest dreams.

THE POWER OF QUESTIONS

Have you ever had a conversation with someone and come away feeling that they just were not interested in you in the slightest? They seemed to go on and on about themselves, and didn't give you the opportunity to talk about anything that was of interest to you? The chances are that they didn't ask you a single question. Go on, think back to the conversation…. try and recall the questions that they asked you? Better still, make a note to count the number of questions that you are asked in the next major conversation that you have.

Questions are a key tool for the individual who has decided to bring success into their life. Why? Because questions require answers, and answers give us information. The more information that you can establish about people, then the easier it is to work out how you can help them, and how they can help you to achieve your respective goals. I remember when I first started out in training. One of the very first sessions I did sticks in my mind. I had decided that it would be an excellent idea if I gave the lucky delegates a brief overview of my amazing background and qualifications, in order to establish my credibility as a person worthy of their attention. I cringe when I recall how I stood, firmly clasping a lectern, rabbiting on for about twenty minutes, boring them rigid with the smallest details of my varied career to date.

A few years later, I was invited to attend an accreditation centre, run by an American company. The purpose of the centre was to become licensed to deliver a set of their programmes. They introduced everyone to a whole new way of training, calling it facilitation. The key thing about facilitation, as far as I could work out, was that it had one golden rule at its core.

Whenever you feel yourself wanting to tell them something, stop and ask a question.

I can safely say that this simple rule dramatically changed the results of my sessions overnight. All of a sudden I was faced with groups of interested and engaged delegates who almost ran the sessions for themselves, uncovering the key learning points as they went along. Amazing.

The power of questions can have a dramatic effect on the way that you live your life. So, when was the last time you asked a question, and what was it? One common denominator with people who are continuously accomplishing their planned objectives (which mean something to them), seems to be their desire to ask questions. They seem to be curious about everything, and have an almost insatiable appetite for finding out about things.

What happens when we fail to ask questions? Well it can turn a relatively straightforward situation into something of a nightmare. People generally try and fill in the blanks themselves by assuming. This is a dangerous process, because we can so easily get hold of the wrong end of the stick. So what types of questions are there and when should we use them?

There are two basic types of questions, 'open' and 'closed'. The former will generally get you more information than the latter. An open question is one that elicits information. Open questions generally start with the adverbs —

How, Why, When, Where, Who, What,

I.e. 'How did you become to be a motivational speaker and coach?' 'What qualifications do you have to help you in this occupation?'

Closed questions can, on the other hand, can generally be answered with either a simple 'yes' or 'no'. They are best used to clarify or confirm detail.

I.e. 'So you have a Diploma in Performance Coaching?' 'Yes.'

A combination of open and closed questions will give you an amazing amount of information and detail. Not only that, you will find that people will begin to view you in a positive and favourable light, because you appear to be interested in them. After all, by asking questions you are invariably allowing them to talk about their favourite subject, which is themselves.

In order that your newfound questioning skills are seen as a natural part of your conversational ability, it is vital that you combine them with effective listening. This means that you are totally focussed on the other person, maintaining eye contact and really listening to the responses that they are making. When they have finished speaking, it is a great idea to allow a two second pause, before you start speaking. This allows you to know that they have really finished, (after all there is nothing worse than someone who talks over the end of your sentences is there?), plus it gives you some thinking time to absorb what they have said and to make an appropriate response. Pick up on the key themes of their conversation by asking open questions that relate to what they have mentioned. You will be amazed by the positive responses and reactions that this will encourage in other people. You will become a far more effective and efficient communicator, which is a key skill for high–achieving individuals.

Set yourself a challenge. Over the next few days, resolve to ask more questions in all of your conversations. Be careful not to overdo it! Too may questions in series can become almost like an interrogation for the other person. However, make a conscious effort to introduce them into your everyday speech. Focus hard on the two–second–pause rule, and reap the benefits of one of the simplest, yet most underused skill that we have as human beings. One final question. This is one that I would encourage you to ask of yourselves as often as you can. It can be applied to every aspect of your life. Simply ask — 'Why not?'

In the search for answers to this question you will encourage yourself to challenge situations and events that would otherwise have presented as insurmountable obstacles or unachievable goals. 'Why not?' encourages us to look for different ways of doing things and gives us the motivation to go on and achieve those planned objectives which are central to our progress as goal–orientated, meaningful specifics.

BODY TALK

You just know, don't you, whether you like someone or not? When we are introduced to someone for the first time, we make instant decisions about them based on the things we observe. It might be their accent, for example. But they don't even have to speak, do they, and yet we start to judge them and put them into categories? It might be the way they are dressed, or their hairstyle, or the fragrance that they possess. There is an expression, which says — 'You never get a second chance to make a first impression'.
I think that is absolutely true. First impressions are a little bit like sticking your hands in a bowl of quick drying cement. If you put your hands in, and then take them out, you leave an impression, which can set within minutes. Once the cast is 'formed', then it is virtually impossible to alter.

It would make sense then, if we are looking to create a positive (and lasting) first impression, that we think about some basic pointers with regards to body talk. I remember being introduced to a multi–(dollar) millionaire at a friend's wedding some years ago. He was an American who had made his money through a multi–level marketing company. I was really curious as to how he had become a millionaire and plucked up the courage to go across the room and introduce myself to him. As I approached him, all I could focus on was the huge diamond ring that he was wearing. The light kept hitting it and sending reflections everywhere, like one of those huge rotating disco mirror balls!

I introduced myself something like this —
'Excuse me Mr Gulluick, my name is Neil,' (offering my hand) 'and I just wanted to ask you a question. How did you become such a wealthy man? What would you say was the one key secret to your success?'
I was absolutely stunned by his response!
'Sir, he said (they are so polite those Americans!) You've just done exactly it?'
A little bemused by this, I enquired exactly what he meant by this. He proceeded to tell me that he firmly believed that the secret to success in all walks of life, was the ability to walk up to someone (even complete strangers), smile, shake them firmly by the hand, and look them squarely in

the eye, whilst introducing yourself clearly and succinctly. That simple act impresses people the world over.

Yet we don't do it, do we? How many times have you been introduced to someone who fails to look you in the eye, whose face would probably crack if they smiled, whose handshake was a little bit like grapping hold of a piece of wet fish, and who mumbles their name inaudibly so that you haven't got the first clue who they are or what they do? Answers on a postcard please.

So what can we do to ensure that we don't fall into this category? Well, there is another expression, which says that practise makes perfect. So why not spend some time practising your first impression? Have a look at your smile in a mirror. Do you look genuine? Do you smile with your eyes? For me, this is the only indicator of a genuine smile. If you think that's nonsense then glance through some magazines searching for pictures of Victoria Beckham. She is without doubt the queen of the forced smile. Better still, come closer to home by trawling through your photo collection, and see what you can come up with!

I can't help but chuckle when I visit my local Post Office. They currently have a leaflet on display advertising some service or other. The reason why it makes me laugh is that there is a huge picture of the TV 'personality' Chris Tarrant on the front. They must have caught him on a bad day, because Chris has the biggest, forced and most insincere smile that I have ever seen make it to print. He literally looks like a grinning idiot. The thing that really makes me laugh is that, if this was the best print from the photo-shoot, what must the rest have been like!

Making eye contact is also crucial to the process of sincerity. It has been said that the eyes are the gateway to the soul. They leak so much of our emotion and true feelings. Think how unnerving it is when someone does not make eye contact with you. I can remember a lecturer at Leicester University who would come into the room, put his bag down, turn to face the window, and proceed to talk to the outside world for an hour. He never once made eye contact with anyone in the room! Very bizarre!

Another key feature of 'switched on' people, is that they live life 'in the moment' and are very much 'there'. You know that this is the case, because when you talk to such people, they maintain eye contact and look as if they are interested in what you have to say. They also listen intently. We learn nothing when we are talking. It is only when we shut up and listen, that we give ourselves the opportunity to learn something new. The word 'listen' is itself an anagram of the word 'silent'. Perhaps that should be our biggest clue!

So remember, smile with your eyes, give a firm handshake, make and maintain eye contact and, perhaps most important of all, stop talking and start listening.

MIND YOUR LANGUAGE

Sometimes it can be just word, can't it? You are sailing along nicely, and then for some reason, the conversation takes a turn for the worst. I remember my wife and I were out for a walk one day. We were having a very pleasant stroll through the Staffordshire countryside, when we came upon the signs for a country hotel. As it was approaching lunchtime, we thought we might call in and have a bite to eat. We walked up the long drive to the hotel, went in through the impressive front door and approached reception. There were two women behind the desk and they seemed to be deep in consultation studying a roster of some kind. Eventually, after a few moments, one of the women looked up, gave us a cursory glance and asked —

'Can I help you?'

'Yes, I hope you can,' I replied, 'We would like to have some lunch thanks.'

'I'm sorry sir,' came the reply, accompanied with a very derogatory expression, 'we are not open to members of the general public.'

'Oh,' I said, as we turned on our heels and made a swift exit. As we walked away, back down the long driveway, I remember turning to my wife and seeing the same expression in her face. We both felt as if we had been given a mild rebuke. It was that phrase "members of the general public," combined with a slightly snotty facial expression, which contributed to the overall impression that we were left with. Unfortunately for them, the impression was a negative one.

After a couple of minutes walking, I remember feeling indignant and annoyed at the way we had been spoken to. It felt as if we had been to see the head teacher and she had told us off for something we hadn't done! We both resolved there and then, never to go back there, neither would we recommend it to anyone.

Why should the choice of words have had such a negative effect? I thought about it afterwards. Not only was it the choice of words, but also it was the 'body language' that the receptionist was displaying. Now we can do something about the words that we use, however one thing that I have noticed over the years, is that our body language tends to come out 'unedited'. That is, we have little or no control over the non-verbal messages that we give out when we interact with other people. We can certainly try and control it, and generally this will be effective for as long as we are consciously aware that we are trying to control it! However, once we lose that conscious thought and relax into our natural state of being, we soon revert to the unedited version of our 'silent messages'.

So what could the hotel receptionist have said, that might have made us feel as little more comfortable? Well, we had some fun on the way home, coming up with alternatives for 'members of the general public.' My personal favourite was 'the great unwashed', however we decided that the most appropriate phrase in that circumstance may have been —

'I'm sorry sir, we are not open to non–residents.'

At least this would have let us down gently! So, what words and phrases are you using on a regular basis that may be creating a negative impression with other people? No one likes to be around a negative source. They drag you down and suck your very life–being from you. You know the type of people I mean, don't you? They are the ones who generally tell you their life history of chronic illnesses and woes, and all you asked was — 'How are you?'

Here is a great way of maintaining a positive approach. In future, whenever someone asks you this question, decide that you will answer — 'I'm excellent, thanks.' Even if you are feeling like death on a stick, by giving this answer you not only feel better yourself, but you also offer an overwhelmingly positive response to them. Try this out for yourself. You will find that it has a very strange effect, very quickly. You will become known as a positive person, which in turn will attract opportunities. People like to be around and deal with positive individuals. Let's face it; no one likes to be lumbered with a moaner. I call them 'pickled onion people', or POP's for short. The reason is that whenever you come across them, they always have the exact same expression on their faces. It's just as if they have been asked to take part in a marathon pickled onion sucking contest!

Think also about the vocabulary that you are using. If you incorporate positive words and phrases into your everyday conversation, then you will be amazed at the subtle differences that begin to enter your life.

Perhaps the one most important word that you can choose to use on a regular basis is the one that we sometimes have the most difficulty with. That is other people's names! How many times have you been introduced to someone, only to find yourself desperately scrambling around five minutes later, to try and remember something that comes even vaguely near to the name that you have so quickly forgotten! A person's own name is the sweetest sound in the world…to them! So how can we start to remember names?

The first thing to do is make sure that you have heard the name correctly in the first place. This may mean asking them to repeat it. Don't be embarrassed to do this. It has real value. Firstly it demonstrates to them that you are interested in them and are listening effectively. Secondly, the repetition of the name will serve you well as you attempt to lodge the name into your memory banks. If you have the facility, you may want to write down the name as soon as you hear it. The next key thing is to use the name as quickly as possible in the conversation with them. By using the name you will give yourself an inner confidence that you have memorised it correctly. Continue to use the name throughout the conversation on a regular basis (without overdoing it!). This will not only increase your retention but will also lock in their interest. It is a well-known fact that we perk up when we hear our own name!

One method of remembering names is to link the person to the name via some sort of unusual connection. In my case for example, my first name is Neil. You may (as a lot of people seem to do!) make a connection between the name and the process of getting down on your knees. You can then visualise the person on their knees in church for example, or kneeling down in the garden doing some weeding. This kind of mental imagery creates a picture of the person that becomes ultimately memorable and therefore easy to recall.

One final point on other people's names. The next time you are in a shop or a situation where you find yourself opposite someone who is wearing a badge with his or her name on, use it. Call them by their name, and see the reaction that you get! It's absolutely incredible. This works particularly well with first names rather than surnames. After all, why do they wear these badges in the first place? Yet very few people take the time or trouble to make that person feel special by allowing them to hear the most interesting word in the universe. Get into the habit of doing this and you will find that it will generate positive energy within yourself, which goes out into your immediate surroundings and is returned to you with interest. You will also begin to receive better than average customer service!

WHEN WILL I GET TO THE JAM?

These were the words uttered by my son, William, aged four and a little bit, as he tackled a huge doughnut. He had been going at it for ages, gnawing away at the dough like a demented rabbit. What struck me was the look on his face, as he kept on battling through to the core of the doughnut. It was one of frustration, annoyance and disbelief. I think he thought he was going to get a mouthful of jam with his first bite. When he hadn't got any after five or six, he stopped munching, looked at me mournfully and uttered that immortal phrase
'When will I get to the jam, Daddy?'
'Soon,' was my reply, 'just keep on going with what you are doing, and you will get to it eventually.' There was a look of mild disbelief in his eyes, as he went back into combat with the dough. I'm not sure that he totally trusted me that there was any jam in there in the first place!

Then, just at the point where I could see he was going to give it up as a bad job, he struck gold....or rather strawberry, as jam oozed out all over the place!

Have you ever found yourself asking that question, though? When will I get to the jam? The truth is that we are all seeking our own personal 'jam' aren't we? What is your 'jam'? What are you working towards in your life? How far towards achieving your aim are you? Do you know if you are looking in the right place for your jam? After all, you're not going to find jam in a chocolate digestive. How much effort are you willing to put into your jam search? Will you continue no matter what? Or will you give up at the first sign of failure?

There are two key lessons that I learnt that day from William. The first is that in order to set up achievements for success, it is vital to make sure that we are striving in the right direction. Just as William would struggle to find jam in a chocolate digestive, so we must examine our circumstances and situation in order to give us the best and most appropriate chance of success. There is absolutely no use in being halfway up the ladder, if it is the wrong ladder, leaning against the wrong wall. Better still to be at the foot of the right ladder, up the right wall. If we apply that metaphor to our lives, then you might want to clarify that you are on the right path in all aspects of your life. Are you in the right job, company, relationship, marriage, house, country, circle of friends?

Now is the time to take stock and to make those decisions that will place your ladder against the right wall. This will take great courage. It will almost certainly involve upheaval of some sort. Yet, I will ask you one simple question. What will happen if you leave your ladder where it is at the moment? Will you get everything that you are looking for? Maybe. How much more certain would you be of achieving your goals and dreams if you took control right now, and placed your ladder in a different place. A place where you knew there was an increased chance of you being genuinely happy with your life choices? Have the courage to become your authentic self, and take the choices and decisions that mean something to you. After all, it's your life.

The other thing that I learnt from William that day was the power and value of persistence. This has to be one of the most important qualities for achieving goals, over and above any other. There were times when he looked like giving in, and treating us to a burst of tears. Yet, with some gentle encouragement, he kept on going and eventually hit the jackpot.

Thinking about it, I suppose there must have been an element of doubt in his mind as to whether or not there really was jam in the doughnut. After all, some doughnuts he has had in the past were the ring variety, and they certainly didn't have any. However, every doughnut of the size and shape that he was eating that day had previously bore the fruit of internal jam. Isn't life exactly like that though? Sometimes we are not quite sure if the reward will be there for us. Sometimes the effort to get the reward appears to outweigh the reward itself, and we give up. Here is a scenario to think about. Suppose I pulled up outside your residence with a huge empty dumper truck. I then show you a small diamond, less than a centimetre in diameter. This diamond turns out to be worth a cool £1 million pounds. I then fill the dumper truck a third full with fine white sand, before casually tossing in the diamond and then filling the truck up with the rest of the sand. The rules of the game are that you have as long as it takes to find the diamond using only your bare hands. If you get it, then you keep it. That simple.

The question is, how long would you keep searching for the diamond? Undoubtedly I think that most of us would persevere until we found it, no matter what! Why, because the rules are simple and we know that the diamond is in there, because we saw it go in with our own eyes.

What if I simply turned up in front of your house with a dumper truck full of sand, and told you that there was a diamond in there, worth a million quid etc etc. How many of us would start to search the sand, and how many of us would keep going until we found it? Well isn't this exactly like life itself? Sometimes we have to trust that the rewards will be there for us. The only thing that we have to remember is to get stuck in, and keep on going. How many times have you heard stories about people who have given up after massive effort, very often when they were within touching distance of their goal? Be persistent in your endeavours, and, as Churchill famously said —

'Never give up…'

BANANA THEORY

This was an eye–opener. Forget the entire quantum physics stuff and the brief history of time malarkey. When it comes down to it, life is all about bananas.

I encourage you to undertake your own research into this matter. Get yourself along to your local greengrocers, and examine some bananas. I can guarantee that you will find some that are a lovely shade of yellow. This is generally a good indication that the fruit is 'ripe'. You may find that some of the bananas are more of a green than a yellow. This stage in the development cycle is the pre–cursor to ripe and means that the fruit still has some way to go before it is in peak condition. In the greengrocer trade, this is known technically as 'the green stage'. Finally, out back, you may find unsold stock, which has been on the shelves for a couple of weeks! This fruit will have a distinct brown or even black mottled effect on its skin. It has entered the 'rot' stage.

This pattern of green, ripe and rot seems to be universal for all bananas everywhere. So, making the leap, if you were a banana, at which stage of the cycle would you put yourself? Are you green, keen, eager to learn, with a clear path and direction guided by specific goals and dreams? Are you open minded and constantly absorbing information? Or you may feel that you've achieved it all? You've been there, done it, and printed the T–shirt? Nothing more left to do. You are ripe as a ripe thing.

Perhaps you feel that life has passed you by? You are not progressing or achieving anything of any real significance. You long since gave up on setting goals or following any purposeful direction in your life. The rot has truly set in.

Well the good news is that we have a major advantage over the humble banana. We can control our own 'ripening' process by striving to stay out of the rot stage and in the green stage. Hang on, I hear you cry, shouldn't we be aiming for ripe? Well, yes. We should be aiming for ripe, however once we hit the ripe stage there is literally nowhere to go except the rot stage.

Once we think we have been, there, seen it, done it all, then what remains? The message is a simple one. Strive to keep yourself in the 'green' stage. How? By continually setting new goals once your old ones are achieved. Remember that success is not a destination; it's more of a never ending journey. It's the continuous accomplishment of your planned objectives that are worthwhile to you. I believe that the banana theory can be linked to retirement. How many people do you see who work hard throughout their life, aiming for the dream of retirement? Once they actually get to retire, they potter around aimlessly for a few months before passing away? Or retirement becomes a living hell of routine and boredom. These people have entered the rot stage.

If we look at some of the most 'successful' business people and entrepreneurs, then why is it that they continue to work? Most of them could easily cash in their equity and sit idly on a beach all day. Yet they choose to remain in business, some of them working harder than the rest of us put together. They know the value of keeping active and focused. Vow now, to keep yourself green by continually striving to be the best that you can be, by continually setting yourself fresh challenges and new goals, by taking positive action towards your aims. Never retire!!!

There was a farmer. He had just bought a reasonably successful farm somewhere in Wales. The farm had a freshwater stream running through it, which rose high in the mountains and provided a supply of clear drinking water to his herds. One day the farmer noticed that his sheep were gathering around the millpond. This was unusual because they normally drank from the stream high up in the hills. He went out to investigate and noticed that the normal torrent of flow in the stream had reduced to a trickle. Puzzled, he trekked up the hill tracing the stream back.

About half way up, the problem became apparent. A huge boulder had somehow managed to roll down into the stream, almost completely blocking it, forcing the water to gush out over the banks and disperse into the mountain soil. No problem, thought the farmer. It would be a simple enough job to clear the blockage. He sat down to think through his options. Due to the inaccessibility of the spot, it was going to be impossible to drag the boulder out from the stream using the Land Rover. After all the rock was just too big. In fact, the only way to shift it would be to break it down into smaller pieces. But how was he going to do this? He couldn't use explosives, because of the proximity to his livestock?

In the end, he decided that the only way to move it was sheer person - power. He set off back down to the farm and returned with his sledgehammer. After positioning himself up on top of the boulder, he swung a huge hit at the rock. The impact reverberated up the shank of his hammer, shaking his whole body. This was going to be tougher than initially expected. After a whole afternoon of hitting the rock, the farmer returned home blistered, dejected and despondent. He resolved to return the next day and finish the job. In fact he had to return the next day and the next, and the next. Each swing of the hammer did nothing except shatter the silence of the valley with a clinking crack. The surface of the huge obstacle was unmarked apart from a whole series of dents where the hammerhead had made contact.

After a full week of swinging away, the farmer was weary, and, believing the task to be futile one, decided to give up. He returned to the farm and told his wife that they would have to look at alternative water supplies because the natural spring had been blocked. She sympathised, yet suggested that he give it one final go. Reluctantly he agreed, although he knew in his heart that the situation was hopeless. The next day he set off again to the rock. Positioning himself as before, he raised his sledgehammer, and gave it a mighty swing. The head of the hammer came down where it had hit many times before. There was a resounding crack. Then a shudder and a rumble, followed by a searing, snapping sound. The farmer watched in disbelief as the rock sheared into two halves down a perfect split. Each half fell away and the torrent of the stream gushed through and spilled over down the hillside once again.

The farmer collapsed in a heap, exhausted, sore and soaking wet.

So what are you swinging away at in your life at the moment? And are you making progress? Or do you feel like giving up? I'm sure that we've all felt like the farmer at some point in our lives, haven't we? I know I certainly have. After all it will never happen, it's pointless. Why am I wasting my time with this? Why am I putting in so much effort for nothing? Ever felt like giving up? Yes, of course you have, many times. How much easier would it have been for our farmer if someone had come along and said to him?
'It's going to take you 1,023 swings before this rock cracks?'
Well at least he would have known that the rock was going to crack at some stage!

But let's face it, even if we knew how much effort we had to put in, then many of us would still give up, wouldn't we? That's human nature. I mean 1,023 swings! Come on! We all want the easy path, the line of least resistance. Well, sometimes the rock may split on the first or second swing; sometimes you are going to have to keep on, keeping on with no signs of any progress being made. That's the way that life is. Yet was it the final swing that cracked the rock? Or was it a combination of all the previous hits puts together to ensure success?

Many of us give up when the goal is so close, almost within touching distance.

Then someone else comes along, takes advantage of all our efforts, and takes the prize. You've seen it so many times in life haven't you? Well, my final message is exactly that. Keep on, keeping on. Keep on swinging the hammer. Rest if necessary, come back tomorrow, take an occasional day off, yet always return to the task that you set out to achieve and don't give up until it's done. Persistence and resilience in the line of apparent adversity are probably the two key features that define the best from the rest. History is dotted with people who came good, simply because they stuck to the task in spite of everything. Remember that quitters don't win and winners don't quit. Success will be yours if you keep your goals close, and your activity focussed. Because if you want to, and I mean truly want to, then you will.

Good Luck.

INDEX

Affirmations –writing, sharing *19-22*
Action – positive, taking, *28-30*
Attitude – own, positive, *34*
Authentic self *7, 36*

Banana theory *57, 58*
Belief – self *35-37*
Bicycle Wheel of Life – creating *8-10*
Body language *47, 48*
Buzz Lightyear *33*

Comfort zones – recognising, expanding *4-5*
Chinese proverb *28*
Chris Tarrant *48*

Desire 38-40
Decision – definition, Latin roots *38*

Everest – personal *3*
Edward de Bono *4*

Goals –setting, smart method, accomplishment *14-18*

Harry Enfield *32*

Important – definition *24*
Impressions – first, *47*

Jack Black *26*
Jam – when will I get to the, *54, 55*
Jim Carrey *24*
Keep on, keeping on, *59-61*
Life zones *9*
Listening – effective, *46*
Language – minding your, *50, 51*

Meaningful specific 15
Mediocrity 13, 32
Michael Schumacher 14
Mind –conscious, subconscious 19
Money – flow, releasing with joy, 24-27
Momentum –creating and maintaining 41-43

Negativity – recognising, dealing with, 31-34

Persistence – importance of 54-56, 59-61
Pickled onion people 51

Questions – power of, open, closed, 44-46

Resistance – dealing with, overcoming, 31-34

Sabotage 12
Self – authentic 7
Slate – personal 6, 7
Success – defining 11, 12

Talk – self 20
Three P rule 20
To Do list 28-30

Urgent – definition 29

Victoria Beckham 48

Wandering generality 15
Winston Churchill 56

Zig Ziglar 15

BUZZTALKS™

For more information about the range of services offered by
BUZZTALKS™, please visit www.buzztalks.com

I am always interested in hearing your views and opinions on the book and
the impact it has on your life. Please feel free to email me directly at
nhe@buzztalks.com or write to —

BUZZTALKS™
PO Box 1560
Stoke–on–Trent
ST12 9BX

For all enquiries relating to corporate speaking, training, consultancy and
coaching, please email enquiries@buzztalks.com

Many thanks, and my best wishes go to you.
Good Luck once again.

Neil Hawley–Evans
August 2002